A Beginning-to-Read Book

A Visit to the Dentist

by Mary Lindeen

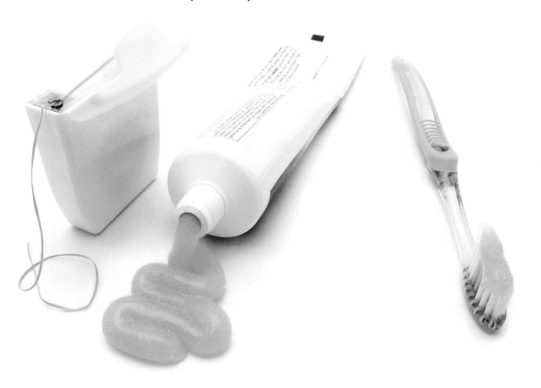

NORWOOD HOUSE  PRESS

DEAR CAREGIVER, The *Beginning to Read—Read and Discover* books provide emergent readers the opportunity to explore the world through nonfiction while building early reading skills. The text integrates both common sight words and content vocabulary. These key words are featured on lists provided at the back of the book to help your child expand his or her sight word recognition, which helps build reading fluency. The content words expand vocabulary and support comprehension.

Nonfiction text is any text that is factual. The Common Core State Standards call for an increase in the amount of informational text reading among students. The Standards aim to promote college and career readiness among students. Preparation for college and career endeavors requires proficiency in reading complex informational texts in a variety of content areas. You can help your child build a foundation by introducing nonfiction early. To further support the CCSS, you will find Reading Reinforcement activities at the back of the book that are aligned to these Standards.

Above all, the most important part of the reading experience is to have fun and enjoy it!

Sincerely,

Shannon Cannon

Shannon Cannon, Ph.D.
Literacy Consultant

Norwood House Press • P.O. Box 316598 • Chicago, Illinois 60631
For more information about Norwood House Press please visit our website at
www.norwoodhousepress.com or call 866-565-2900.
© 2019 Norwood House Press. Beginning-to-Read™ is a trademark of Norwood House Press.
All rights reserved. No part of this book may be reproduced or utilized in any form or by any
means without written permission from the publisher.

Editor: Judy Kentor Schmauss

Designer: Lindaanne Donohoe

Special thanks to Dr. Sanford L. Barr and his staff

Photo Credits:
Shutterstock, cover, 10, 11, 14-15, 17, 18-19, 20-21, 24-25; iStock Photo, title page,
3, 8-9, 26-27, 28-29; Alamy, 4-5, 12-13, 16; Lindaanne Donohoe, 6-7, 22-23

Library of Congress Cataloging-in-Publication Data
Names: Lindeen, Mary, author.
Title: A visit to the dentist / by Mary Lindeen.
Description: Chicago, IL : Norwood House Press, 2018. | Series: A beginning
  to read book | Audience: K to grade 3.
Identifiers: LCCN 2018004465 (print) | LCCN 2018008514 (ebook) | ISBN
  9781684041770 (eBook) | ISBN 9781599539126 (library edition : alk. paper)
Subjects: LCSH: Dentistry–Juvenile literature. | Dentists–Juvenile
  literature. | Teeth–Care and hygiene–Juvenile literature.
Classification: LCC RK63 (ebook) | LCC RK63 .L55 2018 (print) | DDC
  617.6–dc23
LC record available at https://lccn.loc.gov/2018004465

Hardcover ISBN: 978-1-59953-912-6   Paperback ISBN: 978-1-68404-168-8

312N-072018
Manufactured in the United States of America in North Mankato, Minnesota.

It's time to visit the dentist.

You have a checkup today.

You can wait here until it's your turn.

You can play with some toys.

You can read some books.

Now it's your turn.

Climb up in this
big chair.

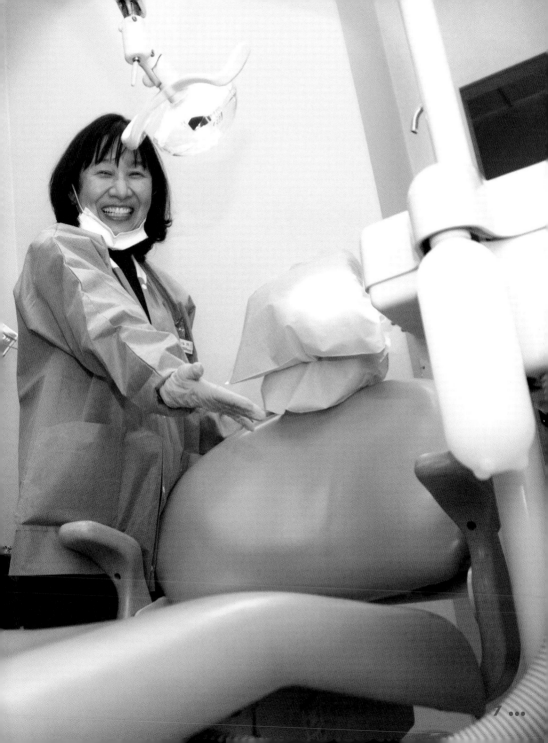

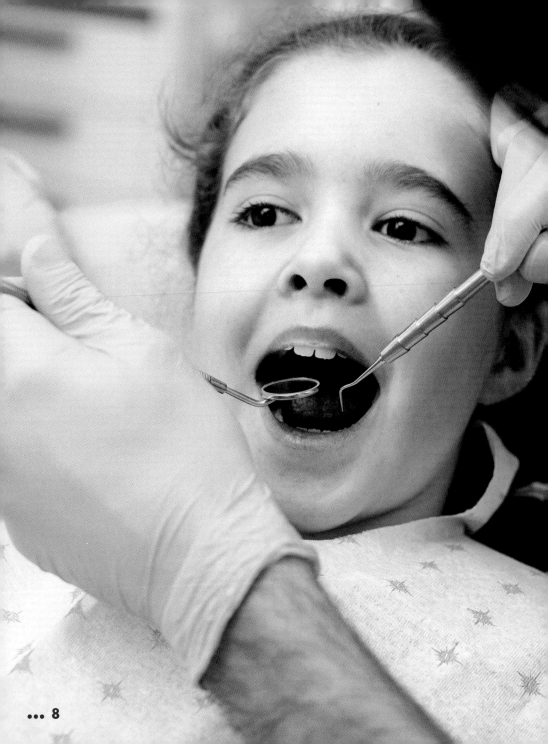

Open your mouth wide.

Let's count your teeth.

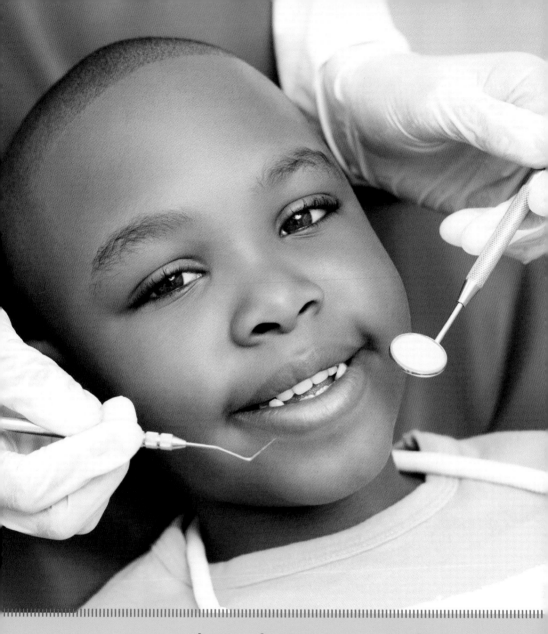

Now let's clean your teeth.

Then you can rinse
your mouth with water.

This is an x-ray machine.

It takes pictures of your teeth.

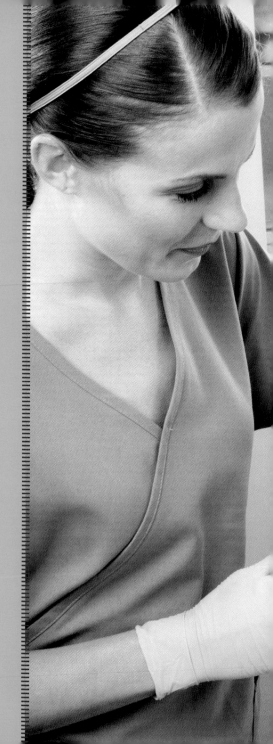

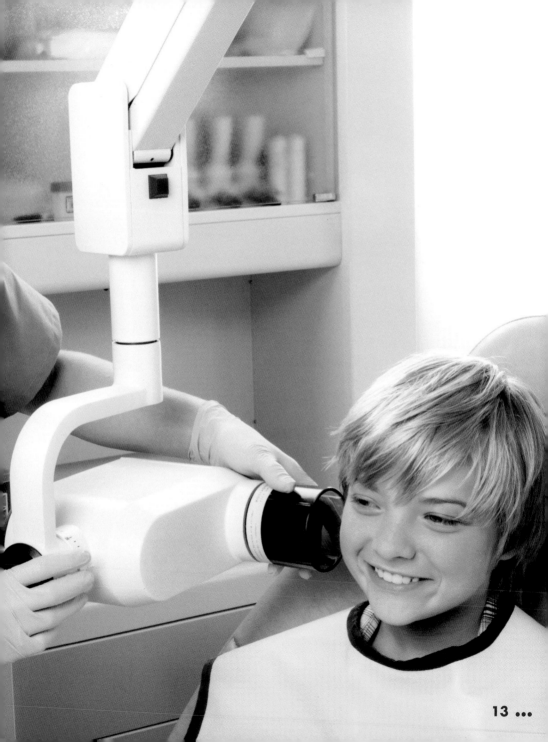

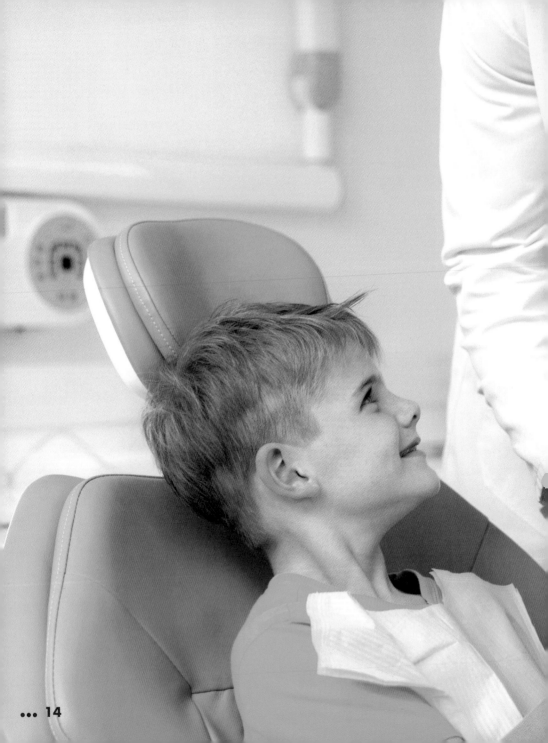

Here comes the
dentist.

He is happy to
see you!

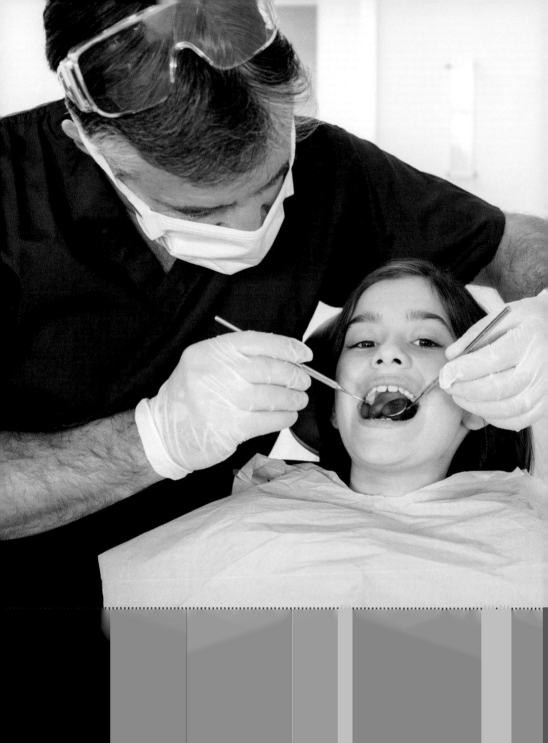

You have a little hole in one tooth.

That is called a cavity.

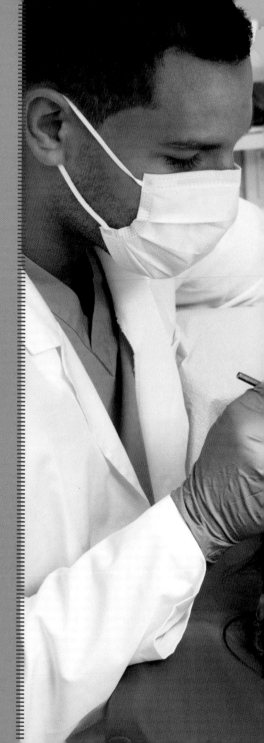

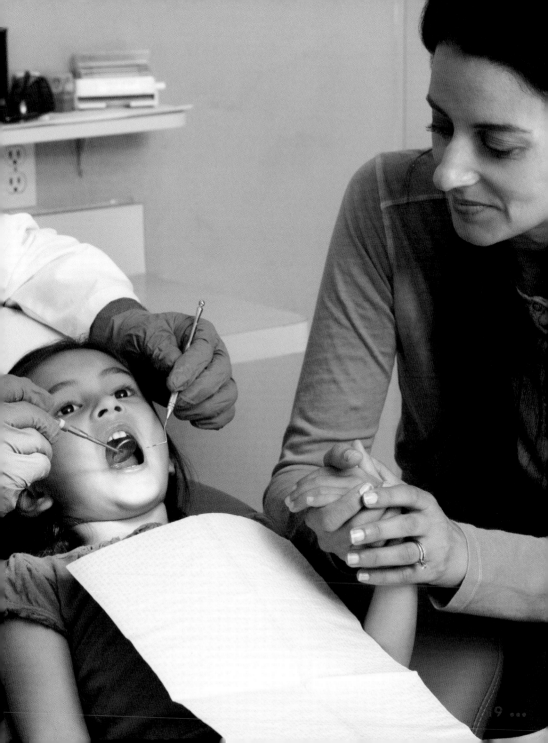

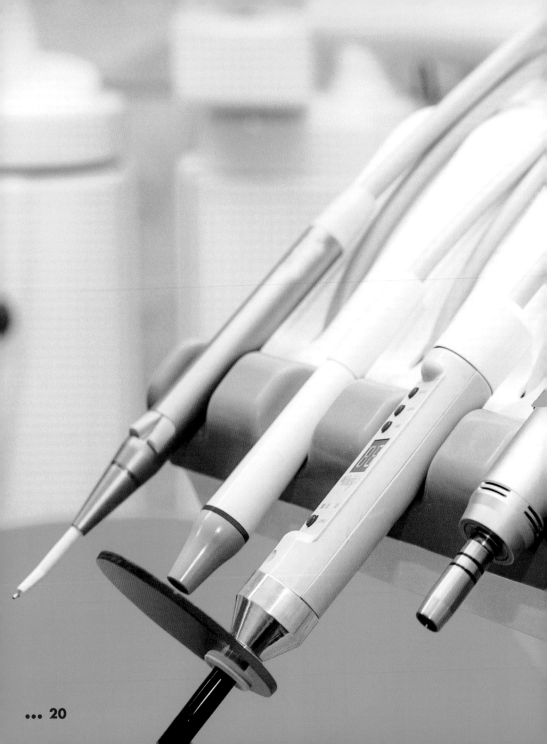

A dentist can
fix your tooth.

He will use these
special tools.

Now your tooth
is fixed.

Look at that smile!

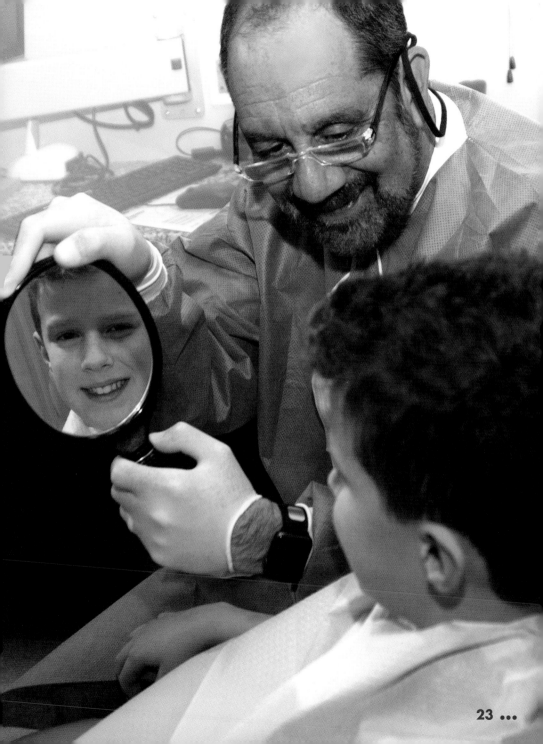

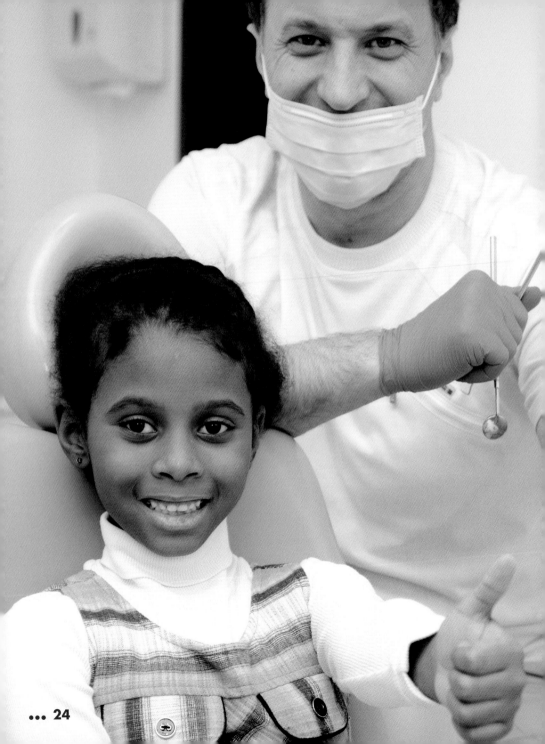

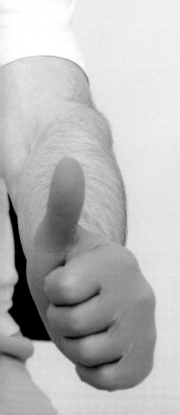

You are all done!

You were a very
good patient today.

It's almost time to go.

But first you get
a sticker.

You get a new
toothbrush, too.

You had a good visit
to the dentist!

...READING REINFORCEMENT...

CRAFT AND STRUCTURE

To check your child's understanding of the organization of the book, recreate the following chart on a sheet of paper. Read the book with your child, and then help him or her fill in the circles with the important events that happen in the order in which they happen when you go to the dentist's office.

1   2   3   4   5   6

VOCABULARY: Learning Content Words

Content words are words that are specific to a particular topic. All of the content words for this book can be found on page 32. Use some or all of these content words to complete one or more of the following activities:

- Help your child make word associations. For example, ask, *How does* dentist *go with* tooth?

- Write the definitions of the words on separate index cards. Have your child choose a card. Read the definition and ask your child to name the defined word.

- Help your child sort the words into different categories.

- Ask your child questions about the word's meaning that begin with *who, what, where, when, why,* and *how.*

- Have your child draw a picture to illustrate the word's meaning.

FOUNDATIONAL SKILLS: Short and long *oo*

When *oo* appears in a word, the vowels can make a short sound, as in *hook* or a long sound as in *roof*. Point to the words below at random and have your child tell if the *oo* makes a short or long sound. Then look for other words with *oo* in reading materials you have at home and have your child read them.

books	looks	tooth	tools
good	toothbrush	too	

CLOSE READING OF INFORMATIONAL TEXT

Close reading helps children comprehend text. It includes reading a text, discussing it with others, and answering questions about it. Use these questions to discuss this book with your child.

- What kind of machine takes pictures of your teeth?
- Why does a dentist want to see pictures of your teeth?
- How do you think you might get a cavity?
- What might happen to your teeth if you never went to the dentist?
- What might happen if a cavity doesn't get fixed?
- How do you feel about going to the dentist? Why?

FLUENCY

Fluency is the ability to read accurately with speed and expression. Help your child practice fluency by using one or more of the following activities:

- Reread this book to your child at least two times while he or she uses a finger to track each word as you read it.
- Read the first sentence aloud. Then have your child reread the sentence with you. Continue until you have finished this book.
- Ask your child to read aloud the words they know on each page of this book. (Your child will learn additional words with subsequent readings.)
- Have your child practice reading this book several times to improve accuracy, rate, and expression.

··· Word List ···

A Visit to the Dentist uses the 86 words listed below. *High-frequency words* are those words that are used most often in the English language. They are sometimes referred to as sight words because children need to learn to recognize them automatically when they read. *Content words* are any words specific to a particular topic. Regular practice reading these words will enhance your child's ability to read with greater fluency and comprehension.

High-Frequency Words

a	get	look(s)	that	very
all	go	new	the	water
an	good	now	then	were
are	had	of	these	will
at	have	one	this	with
big	he	play	time	you
but	here	read	to	your
called	in	see	too	
can	is	she	until	
come(s)	it	some	up	
first	little	take(s)	use	

Content Words

almost	count	let's	smile	toothbrush
books	dentist	machine	special	toys
cavity	done	mouth	sticker	turn
chair	fix(ed)	open	teeth	visit
checkup	happy	patient	today	wait
clean	hole	pictures	tools	wide
climb	it's	rinse	tooth	x-ray

··· About the Author

Mary Lindeen is a writer, editor, parent, and former elementary school teacher. She has written more than 100 books for children and edited many more. She specializes in early literacy instruction and books for young readers, especially nonfiction.

··· About the Advisor

Dr. Shannon Cannon is an elementary school teacher in Sacramento, California. She has served as a teacher educator in the School of Education at UC Davis, where she also earned her Ph.D. in Language, Literacy, and Culture. As a member of the clinical faculty, she supervised pre-service teachers and taught elementary methods courses in reading, effective teaching, and teacher action research.